EMMANUEL JOSEPH

Harmony of Transformation, A Comprehensive Approach to Health, Wealth, and Interpersonal Dynamics

Copyright © 2025 by Emmanuel Joseph

All rights reserved. No part of this publication may be reproduced, stored or transmitted in any form or by any means, electronic, mechanical, photocopying, recording, scanning, or otherwise without written permission from the publisher. It is illegal to copy this book, post it to a website, or distribute it by any other means without permission.

First edition

This book was professionally typeset on Reedsy. Find out more at reedsy.com

Contents

1	Chapter 1: The Dawn of Self-Awareness	1
2	Chapter 2: The Pillars of Physical Health	3
3	Chapter 3: The Mind-Body Connection	5
4	Chapter 4: Financial Well-Being: Building a Solid Foundation	7
5	Chapter 5: The Art of Mindful Spending	9
6	Chapter 6: The Path to Financial Independence	11
7	Chapter 7: Interpersonal Dynamics: The Power of Connection	13
8	Chapter 8: Navigating Conflict with Grace	15
9	Chapter 9: The Role of Emotional Intelligence	17
10	Chapter 10: The Journey of Personal Growth	19
11	Chapter 11: The Intersection of Health and Wealth	21
12	Chapter 12: Cultivating a Growth-Oriented Mindset	23
13	Chapter 13: The Power of Positive Habits	25
14	Chapter 14: The Importance of Giving Back	27
15	Chapter 15: Embracing the Journey of Transformation	29

1

Chapter 1: The Dawn of Self-Awareness

In the quiet moments of reflection, we often find the seeds of transformation. Self-awareness, the cornerstone of personal growth, awakens us to our true potential. It is within this awareness that we begin to understand our strengths and weaknesses, recognizing the patterns that shape our lives. This chapter explores the journey of self-discovery, emphasizing the importance of introspection in achieving holistic well-being. By delving deep into our thoughts and emotions, we pave the way for meaningful change and a harmonious existence.

Our journey starts with understanding that self-awareness is not just a fleeting realization but a continuous process. This process involves taking a step back from the hustle and bustle of everyday life and reflecting on our actions, thoughts, and emotions. It's about asking ourselves the tough questions and being honest in our answers. What motivates us? What holds us back? By exploring these questions, we gain insights into our behavioral patterns and the factors that influence them. This newfound clarity allows us to make conscious choices that align with our true selves.

As we cultivate self-awareness, we begin to see the interconnectedness of our experiences. We recognize how our past shapes our present and how our present decisions influence our future. This understanding empowers us to break free from limiting beliefs and habits that no longer serve us. By embracing our authentic selves, we open the door to personal growth and transformation. Self-awareness becomes the compass that guides us toward a more fulfilling and meaningful life.

The journey of self-awareness is not without its challenges. It requires vulnerability and the willingness to confront our fears and insecurities. However, it is through this process that we find the strength to overcome obstacles and create positive change. By embracing self-awareness, we embark on a journey of continuous growth and self-improvement. It is the dawn of a new beginning, where we awaken to our true potential and embrace the harmony of transformation.

2

Chapter 2: The Pillars of Physical Health

Our bodies, intricate and resilient, are the vessels through which we experience life. Maintaining physical health is not merely about avoiding illness but fostering vitality and energy. This chapter delves into the fundamental aspects of physical well-being, including nutrition, exercise, and rest. By adopting a balanced approach to these elements, we can enhance our overall health and prevent chronic conditions. The pursuit of physical fitness becomes a journey of self-care, where each choice contributes to a stronger, more vibrant body.

Nutrition plays a pivotal role in our overall health. A diet rich in whole foods, such as fruits, vegetables, lean proteins, and whole grains, provides the essential nutrients our bodies need to function optimally. Hydration is equally important, as water supports various bodily functions and aids in detoxification. By making mindful choices about what we consume, we fuel our bodies with the energy required to thrive.

Exercise is another crucial pillar of physical health. Regular physical activity not only strengthens our muscles and bones but also boosts our cardiovascular health and mental well-being. Whether it's through aerobic exercises, strength training, or flexibility workouts, staying active is essential for maintaining a healthy body. The key is to find activities we enjoy, making exercise a sustainable and enjoyable part of our daily routine.

Rest and recovery are often overlooked but are vital components of physical health. Adequate sleep allows our bodies to repair and rejuvenate, while relaxation techniques, such as meditation and deep breathing, help manage stress. By prioritizing rest, we support our immune system and improve our overall well-being. Embracing a holistic approach to physical health ensures that we nurture our bodies, enabling us to lead vibrant and fulfilling lives.

3

Chapter 3: The Mind-Body Connection

The symbiotic relationship between our minds and bodies is a testament to the interconnectedness of our being. This chapter explores the profound impact that mental health has on physical well-being and vice versa. Stress, anxiety, and emotional turmoil can manifest as physical symptoms, while a healthy body can bolster mental resilience. By understanding and nurturing this connection, we can achieve a state of balance and harmony, where both mind and body thrive in unison.

Mental health plays a significant role in our overall well-being. Practices such as mindfulness, meditation, and cognitive-behavioral techniques can help us manage stress and improve our emotional health. By cultivating a positive mindset and developing coping strategies, we enhance our ability to navigate life's challenges with grace and resilience.

Physical health, in turn, influences our mental state. Regular exercise releases endorphins, which are natural mood boosters. A balanced diet provides the nutrients necessary for optimal brain function, while adequate sleep supports cognitive processes and emotional regulation. By taking care of our physical health, we create a strong foundation for mental well-being.

The mind-body connection is also evident in the practice of holistic therapies, such as yoga and tai chi. These practices emphasize the integration of physical movement, breath control, and mental focus, promoting a sense of harmony and balance. By embracing the interconnectedness of our minds and bodies, we foster a holistic approach to health that supports our overall well-being.

4

Chapter 4: Financial Well-Being: Building a Solid Foundation

Financial stability is a key component of a harmonious life. This chapter examines the principles of sound financial management, from budgeting and saving to investing and planning for the future. By cultivating a mindset of abundance and making informed financial decisions, we can create a foundation of security and peace of mind. Financial well-being is not just about wealth accumulation but also about achieving a sense of control and freedom in our financial lives.

Budgeting is the cornerstone of financial well-being. By creating a detailed budget, we gain a clear understanding of our income and expenses, allowing us to allocate resources effectively. Saving is equally important, as it provides a safety net for unforeseen circumstances and enables us to achieve our financial goals. Establishing an emergency fund is a crucial step in building financial security.

Investing is another essential aspect of financial management. By making informed investment decisions, we can grow our wealth and secure our financial future. It's important to diversify our investment portfolio to mitigate risks and maximize returns. Seeking professional advice can help us navigate the complexities of investing and make sound financial choices.

Planning for the future involves setting financial goals and creating a roadmap to achieve them. This includes retirement planning, estate planning, and insurance coverage. By taking a proactive approach to financial management, we can ensure that we are prepared for life's uncertainties and can enjoy a secure and fulfilling future.

5

Chapter 5: The Art of Mindful Spending

In a world driven by consumerism, mindful spending emerges as a powerful antidote to financial stress. This chapter explores the philosophy of intentional consumption, where every purchase aligns with our values and goals. By prioritizing needs over wants and practicing gratitude for what we have, we can avoid the pitfalls of impulsive spending. Mindful spending fosters a healthier relationship with money, allowing us to enjoy the fruits of our labor without compromising our financial future.

Mindful spending begins with awareness. By tracking our spending habits, we gain insights into our financial behavior and can identify areas for improvement. Creating a spending plan helps us allocate resources to what truly matters, ensuring that our financial decisions align with our priorities and values.

Practicing gratitude is another key aspect of mindful spending. By appreciating what we have, we reduce the desire for unnecessary purchases and cultivate a sense of contentment. This shift in mindset allows us to focus on experiences and relationships rather than material possessions, leading to greater fulfillment and well-being.

Mindful spending also involves making conscious choices about the impact of our purchases. By supporting ethical and sustainable businesses, we contribute to positive social and environmental change. This alignment of our financial decisions with our values creates a sense of purpose and integrity, enriching our lives and fostering a sense of harmony.

6

Chapter 6: The Path to Financial Independence

Achieving financial independence is a journey that requires discipline, patience, and strategic planning. This chapter delves into the steps necessary to attain this goal, from eliminating debt and building an emergency fund to investing wisely and generating passive income. Financial independence empowers us to make choices based on our desires and passions rather than financial constraints. It is a path to freedom that allows us to live life on our own terms.

Eliminating debt is the first crucial step toward financial independence. By prioritizing debt repayment and avoiding unnecessary borrowing, we can free ourselves from the burden of interest payments and financial stress. Developing a debt repayment plan and sticking to it requires discipline and perseverance but ultimately leads to financial freedom.

Building an emergency fund is another essential step. An emergency fund provides a financial cushion for unexpected expenses, such as medical emergencies or job loss. By setting aside a portion of our income each month, we can gradually build a fund that offers peace of mind and financial security.

Investing wisely is key to growing our wealth and achieving financial independence. Diversifying our investment portfolio and seeking professional advice can help us make informed decisions and maximize returns.

Generating passive income through investments, such as dividends, rental income, or side businesses, further enhances our financial stability and brings us closer to independence.

7

Chapter 7: Interpersonal Dynamics: The Power of Connection

Human connections are the bedrock of a fulfilling life. This chapter explores the importance of cultivating healthy relationships, both personally and professionally. Communication, empathy, and mutual respect are the cornerstones of strong interpersonal dynamics. By fostering genuine connections, we create a support system that enriches our lives and provides a sense of belonging. The power of connection lies in its ability to uplift and inspire us, propelling us toward our goals.

Effective communication is fundamental to building strong relationships. By actively listening and expressing ourselves clearly, we create an environment of trust and understanding. Empathy allows us to connect with others on a deeper level, appreciating their perspectives and experiences. Mutual respect ensures that we value and honor each other's individuality, fostering a sense of equality and collaboration.

Cultivating healthy relationships also involves setting boundaries and managing conflicts constructively. By establishing clear boundaries, we protect our well-being and maintain balance in our interactions. Addressing conflicts with empathy and a focus on finding common ground helps strengthen relationships and promote harmony.

Building a support network of friends, family, and colleagues enhances our overall well-being. These connections provide emotional support, encouragement, and opportunities for growth. By nurturing our relationships and investing time and effort in maintaining them, we create a rich tapestry of connections that enrich our lives.

8

Chapter 8: Navigating Conflict with Grace

Conflict is an inevitable part of human interaction, but it need not be destructive. This chapter examines strategies for resolving conflicts with grace and compassion. Effective communication, active listening, and a willingness to compromise are essential in navigating disputes. By approaching conflicts with an open mind and a focus on finding common ground, we can transform challenges into opportunities for growth. Harmony in relationships is achieved not by avoiding conflict but by addressing it constructively.

Effective communication is key to resolving conflicts. By expressing our thoughts and feelings honestly and respectfully, we create an environment conducive to finding solutions. Active listening involves fully engaging with the other person's perspective, validating their feelings, and seeking to understand their point of view.

A willingness to compromise is crucial in conflict resolution. By recognizing that both parties may need to make concessions, we can find mutually beneficial solutions that address the needs and concerns of all involved. Compromise fosters cooperation and strengthens relationships.

Conflict resolution also involves managing our emotions and maintaining composure. By practicing self-regulation and staying calm, we can navigate disputes more effectively and prevent escalation. Approaching conflicts with empathy and a focus on collaboration promotes understanding and paves the way for positive outcomes.

9

Chapter 9: The Role of Emotional Intelligence

Emotional intelligence is the ability to recognize, understand, and manage our emotions and those of others. This chapter delves into the components of emotional intelligence, including self-awareness, self-regulation, motivation, empathy, and social skills. Developing emotional intelligence enhances our ability to navigate complex social dynamics and build meaningful relationships. It empowers us to respond to situations with clarity and composure, fostering a harmonious environment.

Self-awareness is the foundation of emotional intelligence. By recognizing our emotions and understanding their impact on our behavior, we can make conscious choices and respond more effectively to various situations. Self-regulation involves managing our emotions, avoiding impulsive reactions, and maintaining control in challenging circumstances.

Motivation is the drive to achieve our goals and maintain a positive outlook. By fostering intrinsic motivation, we stay focused and resilient in the face of obstacles. Empathy allows us to connect with others on an emotional level, appreciating their feelings and perspectives. This understanding fosters stronger relationships and promotes a sense of community.

Social skills are essential for effective communication and collaboration. By developing strong interpersonal skills, we can navigate social interactions with ease, build rapport, and influence others positively. Emotional intelligence enables us to create a harmonious environment where individuals feel valued and understood.

10

Chapter 10: The Journey of Personal Growth

Personal growth is a lifelong journey that requires commitment and continuous effort. This chapter explores the various avenues for self-improvement, from education and skill development to mindfulness practices and self-reflection. By setting goals and embracing a growth mindset, we can overcome obstacles and unlock our full potential. The pursuit of personal growth is a dynamic process that enriches our lives and contributes to our overall well-being.

Education and skill development are key components of personal growth. By continuously seeking knowledge and expanding our skills, we enhance our abilities and increase our opportunities for success. Lifelong learning fosters intellectual curiosity and keeps our minds active and engaged.

Mindfulness practices, such as meditation and yoga, promote self-awareness and emotional well-being. By cultivating mindfulness, we become more present and attuned to our thoughts and feelings, allowing us to navigate life's challenges with greater clarity and resilience.

Self-reflection is another essential aspect of personal growth. By regularly examining our actions, beliefs, and experiences, we gain insights into our behavior and identify areas for improvement. Setting goals provides direction and motivation, helping us stay focused on our aspirations and track our progress.

Embracing a growth mindset involves viewing challenges as opportunities for learning and growth. By adopting this perspective, we develop resilience and perseverance, enabling us to overcome obstacles and achieve our goals. Personal growth is a continuous journey that enriches our lives and contributes to our overall well-being.

11

Chapter 11: The Intersection of Health and Wealth

Health and wealth are often seen as separate pursuits, but they are deeply intertwined. This chapter examines the ways in which physical, mental, and financial well-being influence each other. A healthy body and mind can enhance our ability to work and earn, while financial stability reduces stress and supports a healthy lifestyle. By understanding the interconnectedness of health and wealth, we can adopt a holistic approach that promotes balance and harmony in all aspects of our lives.

Physical health directly impacts our ability to earn a living. When we are healthy, we have more energy, focus, and resilience, which translates into better job performance and productivity. Conversely, poor health can lead to absenteeism, reduced productivity, and increased medical expenses, which can strain our financial resources. By prioritizing our health, we create a strong foundation for financial success.

Mental health also plays a crucial role in our financial well-being. Stress, anxiety, and depression can impair our decision-making abilities and lead to poor financial choices. Managing our mental health through mindfulness, therapy, and self-care practices can help us maintain clarity and make informed financial decisions. A balanced and healthy mind enables us to navigate financial challenges with confidence and resilience.

Financial stability, in turn, supports our overall well-being. When we have control over our finances, we experience less stress and greater peace of mind. Financial security allows us to invest in our health, whether it's through nutritious food, fitness programs, or healthcare services. By achieving a balance between health and wealth, we create a harmonious life where each aspect supports and enhances the other.

12

Chapter 12: Cultivating a Growth-Oriented Mindset

A growth-oriented mindset is characterized by the belief that our abilities and intelligence can be developed through dedication and hard work. This chapter explores the principles of growth mindset, including embracing challenges, learning from feedback, and persevering through setbacks. By fostering a growth-oriented mindset, we can approach life's challenges with resilience and optimism. It is a mindset that empowers us to pursue our goals with confidence and determination.

Embracing challenges is a key component of a growth mindset. Rather than avoiding difficult situations, we see them as opportunities for learning and growth. This perspective allows us to tackle obstacles with a positive attitude and a willingness to learn from the experience. By stepping out of our comfort zones, we expand our horizons and develop new skills.

Learning from feedback is another essential aspect of a growth mindset. Constructive criticism provides valuable insights into our performance and areas for improvement. By embracing feedback with an open mind, we can make adjustments and continuously improve. Viewing feedback as a tool for growth rather than a personal attack fosters a culture of continuous learning.

Persevering through setbacks is crucial for achieving our goals. Challenges and failures are inevitable, but they do not define us. A growth mindset encourages us to view setbacks as temporary and to keep pushing forward. By maintaining determination and resilience, we can overcome obstacles and achieve success. Cultivating a growth-oriented mindset transforms our approach to life, enabling us to thrive in the face of adversity.

13

Chapter 13: The Power of Positive Habits

Habits shape our daily lives and, ultimately, our destinies. This chapter delves into the science of habit formation and the power of positive habits in achieving our goals. By identifying and cultivating habits that align with our values and aspirations, we can create a foundation for lasting success. The key to effective habit formation lies in consistency and incremental progress. Positive habits become the building blocks of a harmonious and fulfilling life.

Understanding the science of habit formation helps us develop effective strategies for building positive habits. Habits are formed through a cycle of cues, routines, and rewards. By identifying the cues that trigger our habits, we can make conscious choices about our routines and create positive habits that align with our goals.

Consistency is key to habit formation. Small, incremental changes repeated over time lead to lasting habits. By focusing on one habit at a time and gradually building on our successes, we can create a sustainable foundation for positive change. The power of positive habits lies in their ability to automate behaviors that contribute to our well-being and success.

Positive habits also enhance our overall quality of life. Whether it's practicing gratitude, exercising regularly, or maintaining a healthy work-life balance, positive habits promote physical, mental, and emotional well-being. By integrating these habits into our daily routines, we create a life that is aligned with our values and aspirations.

14

Chapter 14: The Importance of Giving Back

Acts of kindness and generosity enrich our lives and contribute to the well-being of others. This chapter explores the importance of giving back to our communities and the world at large. By volunteering our time, sharing our resources, and offering support to those in need, we can make a positive impact and create a ripple effect of goodness. The act of giving back fosters a sense of purpose and connection, reminding us of our shared humanity.

Volunteering our time is a powerful way to give back. Whether it's mentoring a young person, assisting at a local shelter, or participating in community projects, volunteering allows us to contribute to the greater good. It provides a sense of fulfillment and purpose, knowing that our efforts make a difference in the lives of others.

Sharing our resources, whether it's through donations or sharing knowledge, also has a profound impact. By supporting charitable organizations, funding educational initiatives, or providing financial assistance to those in need, we can help create a more equitable and compassionate world. Acts of generosity inspire others to give back, creating a ripple effect of positive change.

Offering support to those in need fosters a sense of connection and community. By reaching out to friends, family, and neighbors, we build a network of support that enriches our lives and strengthens our communities. The act of giving back reminds us that we are all interconnected and that our actions, no matter how small, can make a meaningful difference.

15

Chapter 15: Embracing the Journey of Transformation

Transformation is an ongoing journey that requires courage, commitment, and self-compassion. This final chapter reflects on the themes explored throughout the book and encourages readers to embrace the process of continuous growth and self-improvement. By aligning our actions with our values and fostering a mindset of harmony, we can navigate the complexities of life with grace and resilience. The journey of transformation is a testament to our capacity for change and our potential to create a meaningful and fulfilling life.

Embracing the journey of transformation involves acknowledging our progress and celebrating our achievements. By reflecting on our growth and the lessons we've learned, we gain a deeper appreciation for our journey. This reflection also helps us identify areas for further growth and set new goals for the future.

Commitment to continuous growth is essential for lasting transformation. By staying dedicated to our personal development and being open to new experiences, we create a dynamic and fulfilling life. This commitment requires self-compassion, as we recognize that growth is a gradual process and that setbacks are a natural part of the journey.

Aligning our actions with our values ensures that we stay true to ourselves and create a life that is meaningful and fulfilling. By making conscious choices that reflect our core beliefs, we foster a sense of integrity and authenticity. This alignment promotes harmony in all aspects of our lives, allowing us to navigate challenges with resilience and grace.

The journey of transformation is a testament to our capacity for change and our potential to create a meaningful and fulfilling life. By embracing the process of continuous growth and self-improvement, we can achieve harmony in health, wealth, and interpersonal dynamics, creating a life that is rich, vibrant, and full of purpose.

Harmony of Transformation: A Comprehensive Approach to Health, Wealth, and Interpersonal Dynamics offers a holistic guide to achieving balance and fulfillment in every aspect of life. This book delves into the interconnectedness of our physical, mental, and financial well-being, as well as the importance of nurturing healthy relationships.

Through 15 insightful chapters, readers will embark on a journey of self-awareness, exploring the foundations of physical health, the profound mind-body connection, and the principles of sound financial management. The book also addresses the art of mindful spending, the path to financial independence, and the power of emotional intelligence.

With a focus on personal growth, the book encourages readers to cultivate a growth-oriented mindset, develop positive habits, and give back to their communities. Each chapter offers practical advice, actionable strategies, and inspirational insights to help readers navigate the complexities of life with grace and resilience.

Harmony of Transformation is a testament to our capacity for change and our potential to create a meaningful and fulfilling life. By embracing the principles outlined in this book, readers can achieve harmony in health, wealth, and interpersonal dynamics, creating a life that is rich, vibrant, and full of purpose.

www.ingramcontent.com/pod-product-compliance
Lightning Source LLC
Chambersburg PA
CBHW072023290426
44109CB00018B/2322